ABOUT THESE SONGS

From America has come this fine collection of songs, a treasure... naturally music-loving and music-making negro, with his great feeling for r...

The people who made them were mostly slaves, and they sang... of what they believed in most implicitly — the reality of spiritual things.

Many of the slaves were forbidden by their masters to hold religious meetings, but in the darkness, and in spite of the danger, they used to "steal away to Jesus" after their masters had gone to bed.

They were so sure of what they believed, that they wanted others to know about it, and to be helped by it as they were themselves; so they sang, in their magnificent negro voices, and passed on, in these songs, their faith in Jesus. Although they could not read or write, to pass on the message, they would sing it. It is a wonderful story and record which will last for ever.

SOME PRELIMINARY EXERCISES

These songs have curious tricks of rhythm — so, first of all, practise and learn each of these rhythms, counting them in quavers, slowly and then gradually quicker; and you will find this makes the songs easier to play.

Count 1 to a quaver ♪

" 2 " " crotchet ♩

" 3 " " dotted crotchet ♩.

" 4 " " minim 𝅗𝅥

(1) ‖: ♪ ♩ ♪ :‖ as in No. 7 etc.
      1 2 3 4

(2) ‖: ♪ ♩ ♪ 𝅗𝅥 :‖ as in No. 16 etc.
      1 2 3 4 5 6 7 8

(3) ‖: ♩. ♪ ♪ ♩. :‖ as in No. 20 etc.
      1 2 3 4 5 6 7 8

(4) ‖: ♩ ♩ ♪ ♩. :‖ as in No. 24 etc.
      1 2 3 4 5 6 7 8

INTRODUCTION
(SPECIAL NOTE)

These tunes have been arranged mostly in two-part harmony, as simply as possible, to make them playable by even the youngest music maker.

The left hand is entirely in the five-finger position. The chart at the side of each tune, indicates the notes and fingering to be used by the left hand.

In order to keep to this plan the harmony has frequently been slightly altered.

Where a change of hand position is necessary in the Right hand, a comma (?) indicates where this change is made and which fingering to use.

There are no key-signatures, all sharps and flats being placed in front of the notes requiring them.

Eleanor Franklin Pike

NUMERICAL INDEX

1. Steal away to Jesus
2. Deep River
3. L'il Liza Jane
4. Yonder comes Sister Mary
5. Old Black Joe
6. Go down, Moses: Let my people go!
7. I got a robe
8. Old Folks at home (The)
9. Gospel Train (The)
10. So early in the morning
11. O Peter, go ring-a dem bells
12. Were you there?
13. John Brown's body
14. Marching through Georgia
15. My Old Kentucky Home
16. Who built de Ark?
17. One more river to cross
18. Hail! the Crown
19. Go tell it on the mountains
20. Swing low, sweet chariot
21. Walk in Jerusalem just like John
22. Nobody knows the trouble I see
23. Blow your trumpet, Gabriel
24. Heav'n bells a-ringin' in mah soul
25. Ev'ry time I feel the spirit
26. Little David, play on your harp
27. Somebody's knockin' at your door

ALPHABETICAL INDEX

B	Blow your trumpet, Gabriel	23
D	Deep River	2
E	Ev'ry time I feel the spirit	25
G	Go down, Moses: Let my people go!	6
	Gospel train (The)	9
	Go tell it on the mountains	19
H	Hail! the Crown	18
	Heav'n bells a-ringin' in mah soul	24
I	I got a robe	7
J	John Brown's body	13
L	L'il Liza Jane	3
	Little David, play on your harp	26
M	Marching through Georgia	14
	My Old Kentucky Home	15
N	Nobody knows the trouble I see	22
O	Old Black Joe	5
	Old Folks at home (The)	8
	O Peter, go ring-a dem bells	11
	One more river to cross	17
S	So early in the morning	10
	Somebody's knockin' at your door	27
	Steal away to Jesus	1
	Swing low, sweet chariot	20
W	Walk in Jerusalem just like John	21
	Were you there?	12
	Who built de Ark?	16
Y	Yonder comes Sister Mary	4

1
STEAL AWAY TO JESUS

D.C. al Fine

Chorus: Steal away, Steal away,
Steal away to Jesus:
Steal away, Steal away home,
I ain't got long to stay here.

1. My Lord calls me,
He calls me by the thunder;
The trumpet sounds within my soul
I ain't got long to stay here.
   Chorus: Steal away, ... *etc.*

2. Green trees are bending,
Poor sinners stand trembling,
The trumpet sounds within my soul
I ain't got long to stay here.
   Chorus: Steal away, ... *etc.*

3. My Lord calls me,
He calls me by the lightning.
The trumpet sounds within my soul
I ain't got long to stay here.
   Chorus: Steal away, ... *etc.*

Made in Gt. Britain

Copyright © MCMXLVI by Edwin Ashdown Ltd.

2
DEEP RIVER

Deep river, my home is over Jordan,
Deep river, Lord, I want to cross over into camp-ground
   Oh, don't you want to go to that gospel feast,
     That promised land where all is peace?
   Oh, don't you want to go to that promised land
     That land where all is peace?
Deep river, my home is over Jordan,
Deep river, Lord, I want to cross over into camp-ground.

3
LI'L LIZA JANE

1. I knows a gal that you don't know Li'l Liza Jane,
   Way down south in Baltimor', Li'l Liza Jane.
   Chorus: O Eliza! Li'l Liza Jane,
   O Eliza! Li'l Liza Jane.

2. Liza Jane looks good to me, Li'l Liza Jane,
   Sweetest one I ever see, Li'l Liza Jane.
   Chorus: O Eliza! ...... *etc.*

3. Where she lives de posies grow, Li l Liza Jane,
   Chickens roun' de kitchen do' Li'l Liza Jane.
   Chorus: O Eliza! ...... *etc.*

4. What do I care how far we roam, Li'l Liza Jane,
   Where she's at is home, sweet home, Li'l Liza Jane.
   Chorus: O Eliza! ...... *etc.*

(*A South American Tune written as a plantation song*)

4
YONDER COMES SISTER MARY

2. Yonder comes Brother Joseph,
   How do you know it is him?
   Wid de palms of vict'ry in his han'
   (Repeat from 𝄋 to fine) An' de keys of Beth-e-le-hem... etc.

5
OLD BLACK JOE

S. C. FOSTER

1. Gone are the days when my heart was young and gay;
   Gone are my friends from the cotton fields away:
   Gone from the earth to a better land I know,
   I hear their gentle voices calling, "Old Black Joe".
   Chorus: I'm coming, I'm coming,
           For my head is bending low:
           I hear their gentle voices calling "Old Black Joe".

2. Why do I weep when my heart should feel no pain?
   Why do I sigh that my friends come not again?
   Grieving for forms now departed long ago,
   I hear their gentle voices calling,"Old Black Joe".
   Chorus: I'm coming, ... *etc.*

3. Where are the hearts once so happy and so free?
   Children so dear I held upon my knee?
   Gone to the shore where my soul has longed to go,
   I hear their gentle voices calling,"Old Black Joe"
   Chorur: I'm coming,...... *etc.*

6
GO DOWN, MOSES — LET MY PEOPLE GO

1. When Israel was in Egypt's land,
   Let my people go.
   Oppressed so hard they could not stand,
   Let my people go.
   Chorus: Go down, Moses
   Way down in Egypt land.
   Tell ole Pharaoh,
   Let my people go.

2. No more shall they in bondage toil,
   Let my people go.
   Let them come out with Egypt's spoil,
   Let my people go.
   Chorus: Go down, Moses ...... *etc.*

3. When Israel out of Egypt came,
   Let my people go.
   And left the proud offensive land,
   Let my people go.
   Chorus: Go down, Moses ...... *etc.*

4. 'Twas good old Moses and Aaron, too,
   Let my people go.
   'Twas they that led the armies through,
   Let my people go.
   Chorus: Go down, Moses ...... *etc.*

5. O come along, Moses, you'll not get lost,
   Let my people go.
   Stretch out your rod and come across,
   Let my people go.
   Chorus: Go down, Moses ...... *etc.*

6. Pharaoh said he'd go across,
   Let my people go.
   But Pharaoh and his host were lost,
   Let my people go.
   Chorus: Go down, Moses ...... *etc.*

7
I GOT-A ROBE
(Heav'n, Heav'n)

1. I got a robe, you got a robe,
   All of God's children got a robe,
   When I get to Heav'n goin' to put on my robe.
Goin' to shout all over God's Heav'n, Heav'n, Heav'n,
Ev'rybody talkin' 'bout Heav'n ain't goin' there, Heav'n, Heav'n,
   Goin' to shout all over God's Heav'n.

2. I got-a shoes, you got-a shoes,
   All of God's children got-a shoes,
   When I get to Heav'n goin' to put on my shoes,
Goin' to walk all over God's Heav'n, Heav'n, Heav'n,
Ev'rybody talkin' 'bout Heav'n ain't goin' there, Heav'n, Heav'n,
   Goin' to walk all over God's Heav'n.

3. I got a harp, you got a harp,
   All of God's children got a harp,
   When I get to Heav'n goin' to play on my harp,
Goin' to play all over God's Heav'n, Heav'n, Heav'n,
Ev'rybody talkin' 'bout Heav'n ain't goin' there, Heav'n, Heav'n,
   Goin' to play all over God's Heav'n.

8
THE OLD FOLKS AT HOME

STEPHEN FOSTER

1. Way down upon de Swanee ribber,
     Far, far away,
   Dere's where my heart is turning ebber,
   Dere's where de old folks stay.
   All up and down de whole creation,
     Sadly I roam,
   Still longing for de old plantation
   And for de ole folks at home.
   Chorus: All de world am sad and dreary
       Ev'rywhere I roam
       O darkies how my heart grows weary
       Far from de ole folks at home.

2. All round de little farm I wandered,
     When I was young:
   Dere many happy days I squandered,
     Many de songs I sung.
   When I was playing wid my brudder,
     Happy was I,
   O take me to my kind old mudder,
     Dere let me lib and die.
   Chorus: All de world ...... *etc.*

3. One little hut among the bushes,
     One dat I love,
   Still sadly to my mem'ry rushes,
     No matter where I rove.
   When shall I see de bees a-humming
     All round de comb?
   When shall I hear de banjo strumming
     Down in my good ole home?
   Chorus: All de world ...... *etc.*

THE GOSPEL TRAIN

1. De gospel train am comin'
    I hear it just at hand
    I hear de car wheels rumblin'
    And rollin' through de land.
  Chorus: Den get on board, children,
            Get on board, children,
            Get on board, children,
            Dere's room for many a more.

2. I hear de train a-comin'
    She's comin' round de curve
    She's loosen'd all her steam an' brakes
    An straining ev'ry nerve.
  Chorus: Den get on board ...... etc.

3. De fare is cheap an' all can go,
    The rich an' poor are there,
    No second class on board de train,
    No difference in de fare.
  Chorus: Den get on board ...... etc.

10
SO EARLY IN THE MORNING

1. South Carolina's a sultry clime,
   Where we used to work in the summertime;
   Massa beneath de shade would lay
   While we poor niggers toil'd all day.
   Chorus: So early in de morning
              So early in de morning
              So early in de morning
              Before de break of day.

2. When I was young I used to wait,
   On Massa's table lay de plate;
   Pass de bottle when him dry,
   Brush away de blue-tailed fly.
   Chorus: So early in ...... *etc.*

3. Now Massa's dead and gone to rest,
   Of all de Massa's he war best;
   I nebber see de like since I was born,
   Miss him now he's dead and gone.
   Chorus: So early in ...... *etc.*

11
O PETER, GO RING-A DEM BELLS

O Peter, go ring-a dem bells,
Peter, go ring-a dem bells,
Peter, go ring-a dem bells,
I heard from heaven to-day.

I wonder where my mother is gone,
I wonder where my mother is gone,
I wonder where my mother is gone,
I heard from heaven to-day.

I heard from heaven to-day,
I heard from heaven to-day,
I thank God, an' I thank you too,
I heard from heaven to-day.

O Peter, go ring-a dem bells,
Peter, go ring-a dem bells,
Peter, go ring-a dem bells,
I heard from heaven to-day.

12
WERE YOU THERE?

15

1. Were you there when they crucified my Lord?
   Were you there when they crucified my Lord?
   Oh _____ : Sometimes it causes me to tremble, tremble, tremble;
   Were you there when they crucified my Lord?

2. Were you there when they laid Him in the tomb?
   Were you there when they laid Him in the tomb?
   Oh _____ : Sometimes it causes me to tremble, tremble, tremble;
   Were you there when they laid Him in the tomb?

13
JOHN BROWN'S BODY
American Marching Song

1. John Brown's body lies a-mould'ring in the grave,
   John Brown's body lies a-mould'ring in the grave,
   John Brown's body lies a-mould'ring in the grave,
   But his soul goes marching on.
      Chorus: Glory, glory, Hallelujah!
         Glory, glory, Hallelujah!
         Glory, glory, Hallelujah!
         His soul goes marching on.

2. The stars of Heaven are looking kindly down,
   The stars of Heaven are looking kindly down,
   The stars of Heaven are looking kindly down,
   On the grave of old John Brown.
      Chorus: Glory, glory, Hallelujah! ...etc.

3. He's gone to be a soldier in the army of the Lord,
   He's gone to be a soldier in the army of the Lord,
   He's gone to be a soldier in the army of the Lord,
   And his soul goes marching on.
      Chorus: Glory, glory, Hallelujah! ...etc.

14
MARCHING THROUGH GEORGIA

1. Bring the good old bugle, boys, we'll sing another song,
   Sing it with a spirit that will start the world along,
   Sing it as we used to sing it fifty thousand strong,
      While we were marching through Georgia.
   Chorus: Hurrah, hurrah, we bring the Jubilee!
              Hurrah, hurrah, the flag that makes you free!
              So we sang the chorus from Atlanta to the sea,
                 While we were marching through Georgia.

2. How the darkies shouted when they heard the joyful sound,
   How the turkeys gobbled which our commissary found,
   How the sweet potatoes even started from the ground
      While we were marching through Georgia.
   Chorus: Hurrah, hurrah, ...*etc.*

1. The sun shines bright in the old Kentucky home,
    'Tis summer the darkies are gay,
   The corn-tops ripe and the meadow's in the bloom,
    While the birds make music all day.
   The young folks roll on the little cabin floor,
    All merry, all happy and bright,
   By'm by hard times comes a-knocking at the door,
    Then my old Kentucky home, good-night!
      Chorus: Weep no more, my lady,
           O weep no more to-day:
         We will sing one song for the old Kentucky home,
           For the old Kentucky home far away.

2. They hunt no more for the possum and the coon,
    On the meadow, the hill, and the shore;
   They sing no more by the glimmer of the moon,
    On the bench by the old cabin door.
   The day goes by like a shadow o'er the heart,
    With sorrow where all was delight;
   The time has come when the darkies have to part,
    Then my old Kentucky home, good-night.
      Chorus: Weep no more, ... *etc.*

3. The head must bow, and the back begin to bend,
    Wherever the darkey may go;
   A few more days, and the trouble all will end,
    In the field where the sugar canes grow;
   A few more days to tote the weary load,
    No matter 'twill never be light;
   A few more days till we totter on the road,
    Then my old Kentucky home good-night.
      Chorus: Weep no more, ... *etc.*

16
WHO BUILT DE ARK?

* *usually pronounced 'Nor-ah'*

2. Who built de Ark?
   Noah, Noah;
   Who built de Ark?
   Brudder Noah built de Ark.
   Who built de Ark?
   Noah, Noah;
   Brudder Noah built de Ark.
   Look over yonder an' what do I see?
   Who built de Ark? Why
   Noah built de Ark.
   A band of Angels comin' after me
   Who built de Ark?
   Oh, Noah built the Ark.

17
ONE MORE RIVER

1. Old Noah once he built an ark,
    There's one more river to cross:
   And patched it up with hickory bark,
    There's one more river to cross.
Chorus: One more river,—and that's the river of Jordan
   One more river,—there's one more river to cross.

2. He went to work to load his stock.
    There's one more river to cross:
   He anchored the ark with a great big rock:
    There's one more river to cross.
Chorus: One more river ...... *etc.*

3. The animals went in one by one,
    There's one more river to cross:
   The elephant chewing a caraway bun,
    There's one more river to cross.
Chorus: One more river ...... *etc.*

4. The animals went in two by two,
    There's one more river to cross:
   The rhinoceros and the kangaroo,
    There's one more river to cross.
Chorus: One more river ...... *etc.*

5. The animals went in three by three,
    There's one more river to cross:
   The bear, the flea, the bumble bee,
    There's one more river to cross
Chorus: One more river ...... *etc.*

(There are many other verses — as this was evidently a way to teach children about the great flood of biblical days.)

   The last verse is:-   The animals went in ten by ten,
       There's one more river to cross:
      The ark she blew her whistle then,
       There's one more river to cross.
     Chorus: One more river, ... *etc.*

18
HAIL! THE CROWN

19
GO TELL IT ON THE MOUNTAINS
Plantation Christmas Song

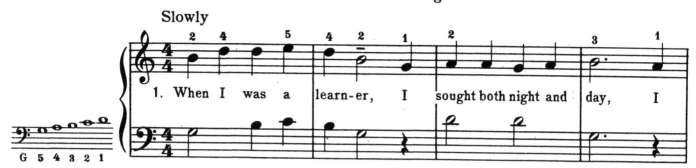

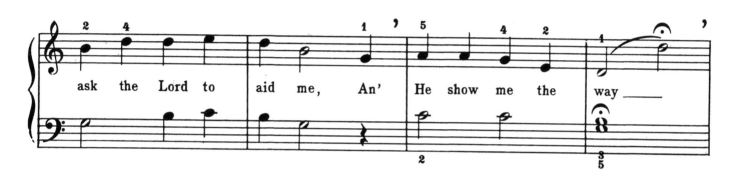

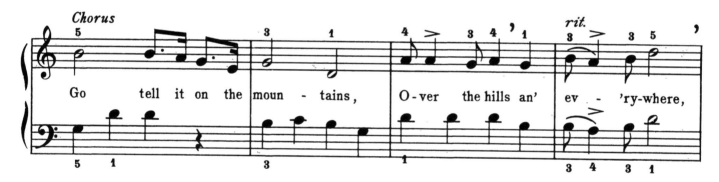

D.C. for 2nd Verse

2. He made me a watchman,
   Upon the city wall,
   An' if I am a Christian,
   I am the least of all.
   Chorus: Go tell it ...... etc.

20
SWING LOW, SWEET CHARIOT

1. I looked over Jordan, what did I see;
   Coming for to carry me home,
   A band of angels coming after me,
   Coming for to carry me home
   Chorus: Swing low, sweet chariot,
         Coming for to carry me home,
       Swing low, sweet chariot,
         Coming for to carry me home.

2. If you get there before I do,
   Coming for to carry me home,
   Tell all my friends I'm coming too,
   Coming for to carry me home
   Chorus: Swing low, ... *etc.*

3. The brightest day that I ever saw,
   Coming for to carry me home,
   When Jesus washed my sins away,
   Coming for to carry me home
   Chorus: Swing low, ... *etc.*

4. I'm sometimes up and sometimes down,
   Coming for to carry me home,
   But still my soul feels heavenly bound,
   Coming for to carry me home
   Chorus: Swing low, ... *etc.*

21
WALK IN JERUSALEM JUST LIKE JOHN

Chorus: I want to be ready,
           I want to be ready,
           I want to be ready,
           To walk into Jerusalem just like John.

1. O John, O John, now didn't you say?
    Walk in Jerusalem just like John.
  That you'd be there on that great day,
    Walk in Jerusalem just like John
      I want to be ready, ...*etc.*

2. Some came crippled and some came lame,
    Walk in Jerusalem just like John.
  Some came walkin' in Jesus' Name,
    Walk in Jerusalem just like John
      I want to be ready, ...*etc.*

3. Now brother, better mind how you step on the cross,
    Walk in Jerusalem just like John.
  Your foot might slip and your soul get lost,
    Walk in Jerusalem just like John
      I want to be ready, ...*etc.*

4. If you get there before I do,
    Walk in Jerusalem just like John.
  Tell all my friends I'm a comin' too,
    Walk in Jerusalem just like John
      I want to be ready, ...*etc.*

22
NOBODY KNOWS THE TROUBLE I SEE

Chorus: Nobody knows the trouble I see,
        Nobody knows but Jesus.
        Nobody knows the trouble I see,
        Glory halleluia!

1. Sometimes I'm up, sometimes I'm down,
       O yes, Lord!
   Sometimes I'm almost to the groun',
       O yes, Lord!
   Chorus: Nobody knows ...... etc.

2. Altho' you see me going 'long,
       O yes, Lord!
   I have my troubles here below,
       O yes, Lord!
   Chorus: Nobody knows ...... etc.

3. What makes old Satan hate me so,
       O yes, Lord!
   'Cause he got me once and let me go,
       O yes, Lord!
   Chorus: Nobody knows ...... etc.

23
BLOW YOUR TRUMPET, GABRIEL

1. De tallest tree in Paradise
   De Christian calls de tree of Life,
   An' I hope dat trump will blow me home
   To my New Jerusalem *(Repeat Verse - then to Chorus)*

   Chorus: So blow de trumpet, Gabriel,
         Blow de trumpet, an' I
         Hope dat trump will blow me home,
         To my New Jerusalem

2. O Paul and Silas, bound in jail,
   Sing God's praises night and day
   An' I hope dat trump will blow me home
   To my New Jerusalem *(Repeat Verse - then to Chorus)*

   Chorus: So blow de trumpet, Gabriel,......*etc.*

24
HEAV'N BELLS A-RINGIN' IN MAH SOUL

2. Walk'd a-roun' from door to door,
   What to do I did not know
   Chorus: O de heav'n bells ......*etc.*

3. I'm a-comin' to de Lord,
   Comin' up till Heav'n I view
   Chorus: O de heav'n bells ......*etc.*

25
EV'RY TIME I FEEL THE SPIRIT

2. All a-roun' me look so fine,
   Ask my Lord if all was mine.
   Chorus: Ev'ry time I feel ...... *etc.*

3. Jordan river chilly and cold,
   Chills the body not the soul.
   Chorus: Ev'ry time I feel ...... *etc.*

26
LITTLE DAVID, PLAY ON YOUR HARP

27
SOMEBODY'S KNOCKIN' AT YOUR DOOR

D.C.

Printed in England